BY MARG RUTTAN

Around My Kitchen Table — TRADITIONS of HOME
By Marg Ruttan

First Printing — May 1993

Traditions of Home Publishing
5134 — 13th Avenue, Edson, Alberta, Canada T7E 1H5

Canadian Cataloguing in Publication Data
Ruttan, Marg, 1949 -
Around my kitchen table
ISBN 1-895292-24-7
1. Life. I. Title.
BD431.R87 1993 081 C93-098102-2

Artwork by Marg Ruttan and Malcolm Pugh.

Designed, Printed and Produced in Canada by:
Centax Books, a Division of PrintWest Communications Ltd.
Publishing Director: Margo Embury
1150 Eighth Avenue, Regina, Saskatchewan, Canada S4R 1C9
(306) 525-2304 FAX (306) 757-2439

Dedication

For my husband Fred who has shared so much of the joy and tears, the laughter and learning, and all the many facets of life and growth that have occurred around our kitchen table.

With love and appreciation for your sharing, encouragement and support.

Introduction

Over the years we pick up bits of wit and wisdom which enrich our lives in numerous ways. Some bits bring a smile and lift our day; some are profound and become vehicles of change; some produce both smiles *and* change. These bits of wit and wisdom often come from everyday discussions around our kitchen table with family and friends.

In looking back at my childhood, growing up in a country home, I realize that life centered around the kitchen. Even after we moved to a major city when I was a teenager, the kitchen was still the heart of our lives. Interestingly, my new city friends seemed to spend a great deal of time in their kitchens, too.

When I grew to adulthood and got married, the focus of my life continued to be the kitchen table. Over the years, it was there that we discussed family issues, the great and not-so-great events of life; where I watched my children develop; where I wrote in my journal (and made numerous discoveries); where I wrote the proposal for my first book, and continue to do much of my writing. Simply, it was, and is, the heart of our home.

Several years ago we moved across the country and at that time we decided to sell or give away many of our possessions. It was then that I became aware that I was willing to part with most belongings, except my well-worn and scarred kitchen table. It didn't take long for me to discover that my attachment to it stemmed from the fact that so much of my life had been lived around its inviting maple surface. Needless to say, it made the trip to our present home. Since that time, in conversations with family, friends and acquaintances across the North American continent, I've discovered that most families' lives are centered around the kitchen, no matter whether they live on the east coast, the west coast or somewhere in between.

During the years I've spent around my kitchen table, and the tables of others, I've gathered many of the humorous and profound bits of wit and wisdom which I spoke of earlier. This little book is the product of those gleanings. I hope that it will touch a responsive chord in your life and provide you with both smiles and provocative thoughts. So, from my heart and kitchen table to yours, may you truly enjoy and be enriched by its contents.

The only person I can change is me.

If you're contemplating giving advice — don't.

Life isn't always fair.

EVERYONE HAS GIFTS AND TALENTS.
DISCOVER AND CELEBRATE YOURS.

Discover that problems are opportunities in disguise.

Be at peace with yourself. It's the first step toward being at peace with the world.

Appreciate the little things.

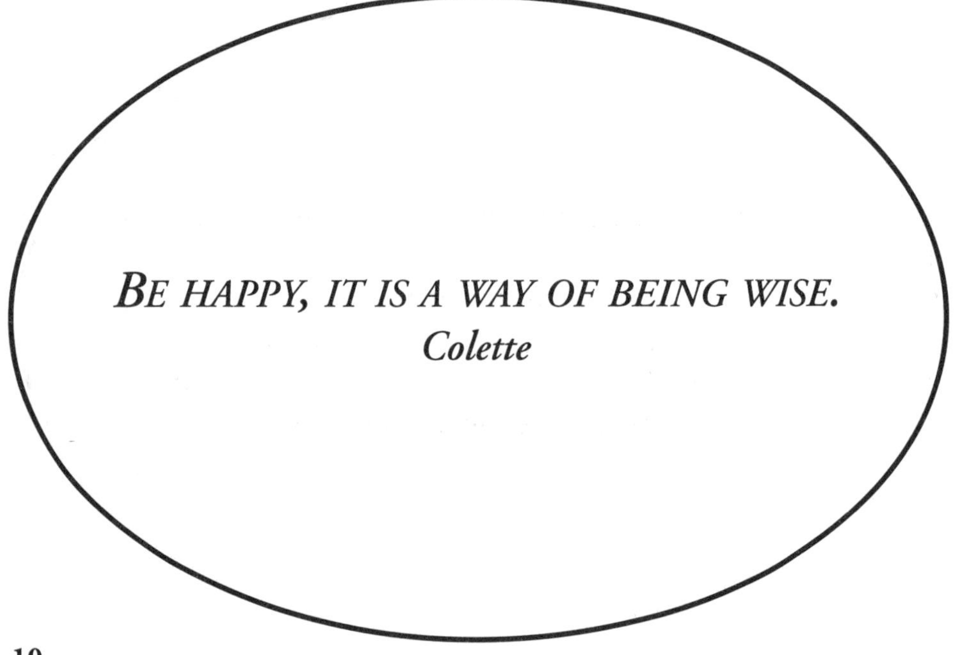
BE HAPPY, IT IS A WAY OF BEING WISE.
Colette

Develop a great sense of humor.

Accept compliments graciously.

There's a direct link between the state of our minds and the state of our health.

Please and thank you really are magic words.

Enjoy each moment.

Most people have more regrets about the things they didn't do than the things they did do.

Keep a journal — you'll be amazed at what you will learn.

There's nothing as cosy as a crackling fire in the fireplace.

Smile, it makes people wonder what you've been up to.

Small children are simply fascinated by garbage cans.

A TEENAGER'S FAVORITE EXPRESSION:
"YOU JUST DON'T UNDERSTAND".

Learn to listen.

We get far better results when we work on improving ourselves than when we work on improving others.

An empty gas tank doesn't get you very far. Neither does an empty mind.

There's no such thing as boredom,
only a lack of interest.

The first step in achieving any goal usually consists
of getting off our butts!

Prunes wrinkle your soul.

AGING SEEMS TO BE THE ONLY AVAILABLE WAY TO LIVE A LONG TIME.

Daniel-Francois-Esprit Auber

Find ten little things to be thankful for every day.

The best toast in the world is made in an old wire toaster, over the embers of a wood fire.

Curiosity makes life interesting.

We all need a hug.

Some people not only close the doors of their minds, they also lock them and throw away the keys.

Read at least one good book a week.

The only people who don't have any problems are in the cemetery.

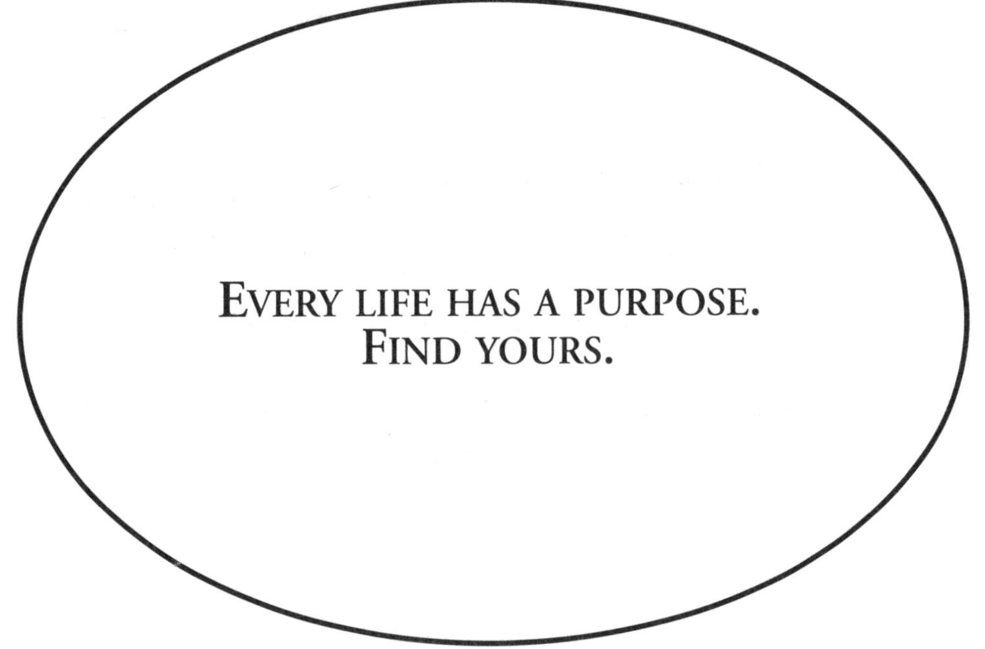
EVERY LIFE HAS A PURPOSE.
FIND YOURS.

Criticize in private; praise in public.

Children are the best teachers of responsibility — they teach you to be responsible for getting them to school, to the rink, to dance lessons, etc. on time.

Nothing smells as good as homemade bread baking in the oven.

Cherish your friends.

Perfection is an admirable goal at work — don't bring it home.

It's a real red-letter day when we can laugh at ourselves.

NOTHING GREAT WAS EVER ACHIEVED
WITHOUT ENTHUSIASM.
Ralph Waldo Emerson

When you start off with “Plan A” in the morning, don’t be surprised if you’re at “Plan E” by evening.

Accept the things you can’t change.

Adults might as well accept the fact that whichever toy Johnny is playing with is the one that little Bobby must have right now.

Teenagers filter out
100 percent of what they
don't want to hear.

People appreciate it when you remember their names and birthdays.

Learn how to change a flat tire.

When your husband tells you he likes chocolate cake, that doesn't mean he wants it every day for the next three months!

A child's first day of school is often as traumatic for Mom as it is for the child.

Actions speak; words whisper.

Worry is suffering tomorrow's possible headache today.

THERE'S A WORLD OF DIFFERENCE BETWEEN "I'M RESPONSIBLE" AND "I'M TO BLAME".

Check smoke detectors regularly.

New ideas and opportunities crop up in the least expected places. Keep an open mind.

Set goals and meet them.

WEAR A SMILE. ONE SIZE FITS ALL.

Anonymous

If we don't risk, we don't live.

Put the toilet seat down.

Don't be surprised if your teenage daughter tells you that mowing the lawn will ruin her reputation. Mine did!

Three-year-olds create the most interesting excuses.

Leave the bathroom sink the way you'd like to find it.

Something good comes from almost every situation.

Eat an ice-cream cone with childlike abandon, savoring every lick.

It's amazing what treasures we discover when we unleash our imaginations.

A flashlight is useless if it has dead batteries.

You only get out of life as much as you put in.

THE ONLY SECURITY THERE IS IN THIS WORLD IS THE SECURITY WE CREATE WITHIN OURSELVES.

You can't be bored without being boring.

Chewing on the end of a pen or pencil helps you concentrate.

One of the most precious gifts we're given is the opportunity to create a fruitful, abundant life.

GENIUS IS ONE PERCENT INSPIRATION AND NINETY-NINE PERCENT PERSPIRATION.

Thomas Edison

A three-year-old's two favorite words:
"Why?" and "NO!".

"If only" are the two saddest words in the
English language.

Discover the joys and benefits of being a volunteer.

A warm bubble bath is a great way to relax.

When you are kind to others, both the recipient and you will feel good.

Don't wait for spring — do it now!

Always return a borrowed dish or pan with a sample of your baking.

BE AWARE OF YOUR THINKING;
IT'S SHAPING YOUR FUTURE.

Honey collects more flies than vinegar;
praise gets better results than criticism.

Knowing and facing the truth
can indeed set you free.

Dishes and laundry are two jobs that are never done.

Getting hysterical doesn't resolve any problems.

My daughter's favorite expression is: "Keep a smile on your face and a rainbow in your heart".

If it's going to be, it's up to me.

WHEN THINGS ARE STEEP,
REMEMBER TO STAY LEVEL-HEADED.
Horace

Laughter extends your life.

Always call and let others know if you're going to be late.

Love is a choice.

Smile lots!

Be enthusiastic.

Cakes rise much better when you remember to put in the baking powder.

Always look into people's eyes when you speak to them. They will understand you better and you will hold their attention.

It's no use complaining; no one listens anyway.

Somebody has to eat the last piece of cake!

Computers eat bytes.

A PARENT'S JOB IS TO BECOME UNNECESSARY.

It's more difficult for some to share other people's joy than their sorrow.

Nurture the child within you; go fly a kite.

Why is it that children always want to give you a kiss when they're wearing chocolate ice cream all over their faces?

WE MAY LIVE WITHOUT FRIENDS;
WE MAY LIVE WITHOUT BOOKS;
BUT CIVILIZED MAN
CANNOT LIVE WITHOUT COOKS.
Owen Meredith

Never criticize yourself openly — others will follow suit.

When we give up doing things because of what other people might think and start doing them because we want to, we are on the road to a wiser, better life.

Why is it that husbands so often lose keys, caps, and glasses?

Any house where young children live is
usually also inhabited
by little ghosts named
"Not Me".

Jigsaw puzzles are a great cure for insomnia.

Be sure the lid is on the ketchup bottle tightly before shaking.

Keep candles, matches and a flashlight handy in case of a power blackout.

THOSE TALENTS WHICH WE DO NOT CHOOSE TO USE WE OFTEN LOSE.

Enjoy a beautiful sunset.

Just because something's on sale doesn't mean it's a bargain.

Use your barbecue, even in the winter.

MAN'S MIND, ONCE STRETCHED BY A NEW IDEA, NEVER GOES BACK TO ITS ORIGINAL SHAPE.

Oliver Wendell Holmes

Keep a list of books you've loaned and
who has borrowed them.

At least once in your lifetime, buy something
extravagant just because you want it.

It's a real gift when we are always welcome at home
— no matter what we've done.

Don't tell secrets.

It's absolutely true that neither success or failure is permanent.

The most precious flower arrangement you'll ever receive is your first gift of dandelions from your child.

Whistle while you work.

Enjoy each day to the fullest; if you don't agree, try missing one.

It's better to make a decision than to sit on the fence until you topple off.

Appreciate good health.

TO LIVE JOYOUSLY IS TO LIVE WELL.

Learn something new every day.

To know others, first know yourself.

It's easier to explain to a four-year-old where babies come from than to try to explain why the sky is blue.

Treat people the way you'd like them to treat you.

Acknowledge your mistakes, learn from them, and THEN MOVE ON.

Your brain listens to what you say. Don't say negative things about yourself or you'll start to believe them.

THE TRUTH THAT MAKES MEN FREE IS FOR THE MOST PART THE TRUTH WHICH MEN PREFER NOT TO HEAR.

Herbert Agar

Read aloud to young children.

Laughter is sometimes the only way to keep from crying.

Buy crafts from local artisans.

Plant lots of sweet peas for their fragrance.

It's absolutely true that it's better to try and fail than to fail to try.

Give away any clothes you haven't worn in the past year.

Before judging other people, first try walking a mile in their moccasins.

Support a charity of your choice.

There's nothing as contagious as a good laugh.

Listen to your inner voice.

TO LEARN FROM OUR MISTAKES INSTEAD OF CURSING THEM IS THE BEGINNING OF WISDOM.

As we learn to appreciate the magic moments of daily life, our lives become more joyful.

Learn to use a computer; they aren't going to go away.

Let your handshake be as trustworthy as a signed contract.

THERE IS NO ADEQUATE DEFENSE, EXCEPT STUPIDITY, AGAINST THE IMPACT OF A NEW IDEA.

Percy W. Bridgeman

Birch bark makes the most wonderful crackle
in a fireplace.

Homemade chicken soup helps cure a cold.

The more you know the more you realize you still
need to learn.

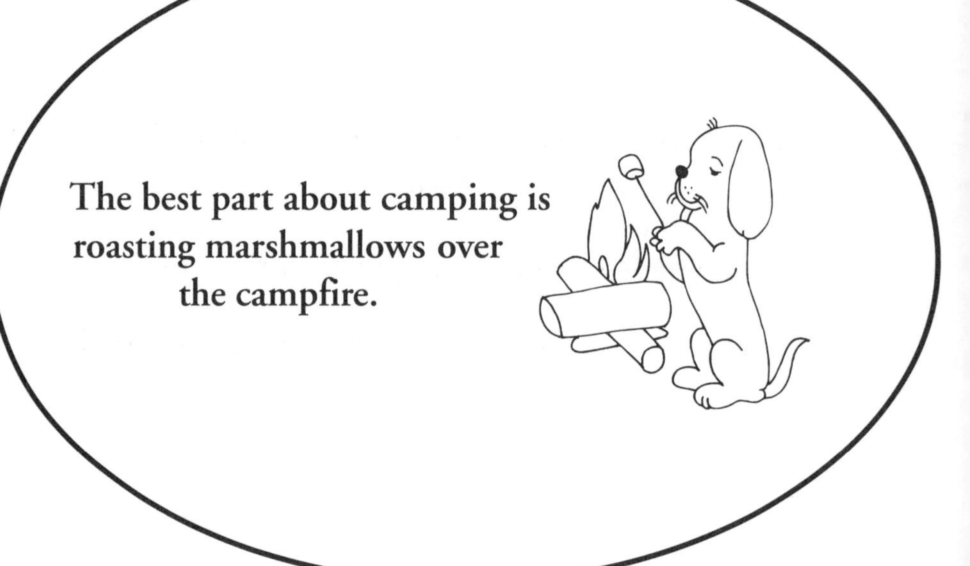
The best part about camping is
roasting marshmallows over
the campfire.

The joy of meeting a difficult challenge is profound.

Quit looking for the pot of gold at the end of the rainbow — start enjoying the rainbow.

If you want to learn the fine art of patience, just undertake a major home renovation project.

TO ABANDON OUR DREAMS IS TO ABANDON OURSELVES.

Help elderly people across busy streets.

If you waste time, you waste money
— time is money.

Find out what you love to do and do it with all your energy. You'll discover the path to success.

Teaching children to eat veggies they're not fond of is easy. Teaching them to **LIKE** those veggies is another matter.

Eliminate the words "should" and "ought" from your vocabulary.

True friends really are Kindred Spirits.

TO THINK IS TO DIFFER.
Clarence Darrow.

You're only as good as your word.

A wise person understands that a problem is simply the seed of an opportunity.

A teenager's version of a clean room gives parents the opportunity to really S-T-R-E-T-C-H their imaginations.

It's said that you can't teach an old dog new tricks, but that's only true if the old dog doesn't want to learn.

Recycle everything you can.

Read *Anne of Green Gables* and other L.M. Montgomery books at least once in your lifetime, for sheer enjoyment.

Plant lilacs outside your kitchen window so you can enjoy their fragrance through your open window in the springtime.

It's said that the early bird catches the worm, but I've seen late evening robins having a feast in our yard.

Don't laugh at another person's problem.

Strive to improve and produce your best — not better another's best.

ONE ENTHUSIASTIC COMMITTED PERSON CAN OFTEN ACCOMPLISH MORE THAN A COMMITTEE.

Choosing to do nothing is still choosing.
Your choice always contributes to the outcome of any situation.

A refrigerator is used to store leftovers until they're old enough to throw away.

We don't have to strive for perfection, but it's a good plan to strive for excellence.

THE WHOLE SECRET OF A SUCCESSFUL LIFE IS TO FIND OUT WHAT IT IS ONE'S DESTINY TO DO, AND THEN DO IT.

Henry Ford

People who hold the same views in old age as they held in their youth have wasted much of their lives.

The only person who can make you feel inferior is you.

The only constant thing is change.

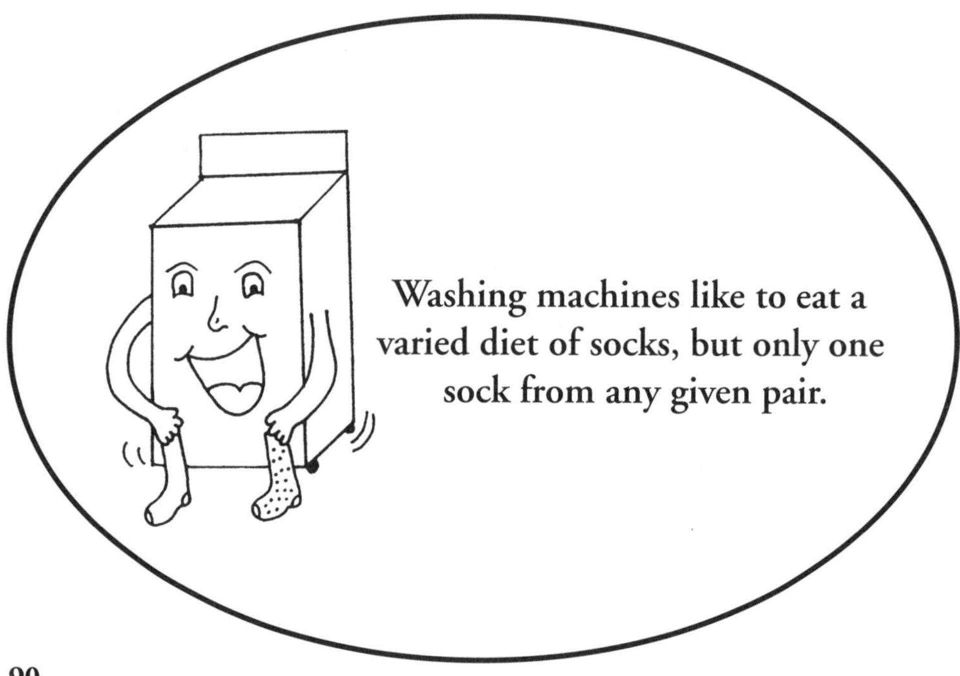
Washing machines like to eat a
varied diet of socks, but only one
sock from any given pair.

We can't change the past but we can shape today.

To live fully requires flexibility.

Why waste energy complaining about the weather?
Complaining isn't going to change a thing.

CHANGING YOUR ATTITUDE FROM "I'LL BELIEVE IT WHEN I SEE IT" TO "I'LL SEE IT WHEN I BELIEVE IT" WILL BRING ABOUT THE DESIRED RESULTS.

Be aware of the wisdom of both the older and younger generations.

We all need somewhere where we belong.

The more we're thankful for, the more we find to be thankful for.

The older our children get the more we realize that some of our great theories were just that: theories.

Own and use a rocking chair frequently.

It is our doubts that develop our faith.

EVERYBODY NEEDS BEAUTY AS WELL AS BREAD, PLACES TO PLAY IN AND PRAY IN, WHERE NATURE MAY HEAL AND CHEER AND GIVE STRENGTH TO BODY AND SOUL ALIKE.

John Muir

Our dreams are a link to our true nature.

Learn to make one entrée exceptionally well, and let it become your "signature" dish.

Return phone calls promptly.

If you tell a young child to pull up her socks, don't be surprised if she does.

It's said that only about three percent
of the population has written goals.
Be part of that three percent.

Don't strive to be right. Strive instead to produce the results you want.

The first person you need to learn to trust
is yourself.

IF THE GRASS SEEMS GREENER IN ANOTHER PERSON'S YARD, IT'S PROBABLY BECAUSE HE USED MORE FERTILIZER.

If you want to get into a creative mode,
try asking yourself "what if?"

A superb marriage is built on a foundation of both partners being accepted for exactly who they are.

Enjoy anticipation. It's half the pleasure of any long-awaited event.

GOD COULD NOT BE EVERYWHERE, SO GOD MADE MOTHERS.

Old Jewish Proverb

Buy quality, not quantity.

If you want to produce good results with kids, the last thing in the world you should tell them is that the results are for their own good.

Keep doing the same things and you'll keep producing the same results.

I've never known a story yet that didn't have two sides, and the truth usually ended up somewhere in the middle.

There's a direct correlation between our self-esteem and our success.

The only limitation on what you can do is what you believe you can do.

Knowledge is what you thought you had before you knew better.

It's important to be in tune with your children during the process of setting them free and making them independent.

Cultivate the habit of being joyful.

Deep personal relationships require total but tactful honesty.

Giving up old roles and moving into new ones isn't always easy, but it's always rewarding.

If you can survive a baby's 2 a.m. feedings, you can survive anything.

Over the span of a few years your child's vocabulary will change from, "Can you give me a ride?" to "Can I borrow the car?"

IT'S USUALLY ADVISABLE TO PUT OUR MINDS IN GEAR BEFORE WE PUT OUR MOUTHS IN GEAR.

If you don't borrow things, you won't have to return them.

As we choose to become responsible for ourselves we become free.

Be your own best friend.

THERE IS NO DUTY WE SO MUCH UNDERRATE AS THE DUTY OF BEING HAPPY.

Robert Louis Stevenson

Things are not always what they seem to be.
Look below the surface.

At least once a week turn off the television and do something different.

Learn to deal effectively with your anger.

Most children have the ability to look particularly angelic and innocent when they've been mischievious.

Learn the rhythm of your body clock and use that knowledge to your advantage.

Nothing warms you up on a cold winter's day like a hot bowl of soup.

Flush!

Kids and grandparents make natural allies.

Many adults still haven't decided what they want to be when they grow up.

Learn that everyone, including you, has the right to say no.

A FEW REDEEMING DEFECTS MAKE US MORE LOVEABLE AND MORE LIVEWITHABLE.

Take lots of pictures or videos.

To truly know ourselves we must see and acknowledge both the shadow and the light. It is then that we begin our journey toward wholeness.

Walk — it's the most beneficial exercise available.

TODAY IS THE FIRST DAY OF THE REST OF YOUR LIFE.

Old Proverb

Exercise your imagination. You'll be surprised at the results.

We always contribute something to any situation we're involved in. Let's ensure that our contributions are always the best of ourselves.

My eyesight isn't failing, my vision's just getting more selective.

When Rover's licking his
chops and Johnny's smiling,
you can be pretty sure
Rover got fed the liver
Johnny didn't want to eat.

Put the cap back on the toothpaste.

We are becoming wise when we discover that success
is the journey, not the destination.

Frequently the faults we dislike in others are faults
we don't want to acknowledge
or recognize in ourselves.

MANY TIMES, WHEN A HUSBAND SAYS HIS MOTHER WAS A GOOD COOK, IT ISN'T BECAUSE SHE WAS; IT'S ONLY BECAUSE HE'S GROWN ACCUSTOMED TO EATING FOOD SHE PREPARED.

I'm not deaf. I'm just choosing not to listen.

Raising children is a real adventure. You're in for quite a few surprises and are often shocked at the results.

The best friend in the world is the one with whom you can be 100 percent yourself.

Water seems to open our creative channels. To get your creativity flowing, try daydreaming while doing dishes or taking a shower or bath.

If you're having a problem in a relationship, look for the changes you can make in yourself, not the other person.

If you can't see to read without your glasses, put 'em on.

HUMOR IS AN AFFIRMATION OF DIGNITY,
A DECLARATION OF MAN'S SUPERIORITY
TO ALL THAT BEFALLS HIM.

Romain Gary

It's said that if you fail to plan you plan to fail.

Creating a great new recipe is just as adventurous as hang-gliding — you're not quite sure where you'll end up in either activity.

If there's doubt — don't.

An apple a day may keep the
doctor away, but a good healthy
attitude helps too.

A pair of old slippers might be comfortable, but a pair of new ones just might point us in some new directions.

Kids and peanut butter just naturally seem to go together.

Liver provides iron, but so do many other far less obnoxious foods, such as raisins and eggs.

WHEN THE JOB YOU DO CONSISTS OF WORK YOU LOVE, YOU AREN'T ALWAYS LIVING YOUR LIFE FOR FRIDAY AT QUITTING TIME.

It certainly makes life interesting when
you have a five-year old who asks questions like,
"Where does the dark go?"

Did you know that a quart of milk, when spilled, can
cover a whole kitchen floor?

What happens to us is far less important than what
we do about it.

You know your child is window shopping when he's standing in front of the fridge with the door open.

New combinations of foods and spices make for adventurous and exciting eating.

Life is like a car. Once in motion, either you take charge by steering and chart your course, or you're likely to end up in the ditch.

THE MOST WASTED OF ALL DAYS IS THAT IN WHICH WE HAVE NOT LAUGHED.

Sebastien R. N. Chamfort

We would be wise to be aware of how effortlessly change occurs in nature and emulate it in the changes in our own lives.

If life has become boring, try playing a different tune in a different key and at a different tempo.

Better to be known for who you really are than for the position you hold.

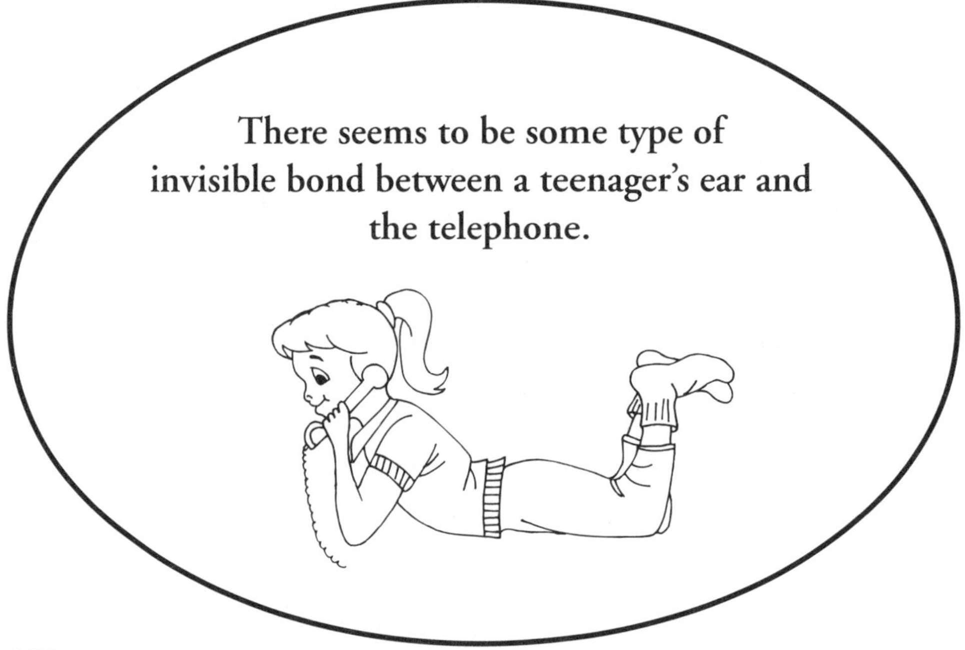
There seems to be some type of
invisible bond between a teenager's ear and
the telephone.

A cute kid can probably worm his way into your heart quicker than a good kid.

We can't very well create a peaceful environment when our inner lives are in turmoil.

Stand up straight.

WHEN FEELING PRESSURED BY TOO MANY TASKS, MAKE A LIST OF ALL YOU HAVE TO DO. THIS CLEARS YOUR MIND OF REMEMBERING EVERYTHING AND FREES IT TO CONCENTRATE ON THE JOB AT HAND.

Men probably wouldn't like being called "the husband" any more than women like being called "the wife".

Learn to pop popcorn.

Laughter and a smile are understood the world over.

THOSE WHO BRING SUNSHINE TO THE LIVES OF OTHERS CANNOT KEEP IT FROM THEMSELVES.

Sir James Barrie

Enjoy life. The joy that you postpone today can't be relived at a later date.

Spring fever is just another way to describe hope — but what a great hope it is!

Go on at least one picnic every summer.

One way to pick yourself up if you're feeling down is to wear bright, cheerful colors.

Learn to forgive yourself.

There's nothing quite so precious as a baby's smile.

When your children get to be around ten years of age, don't be surprised to discover that they view 20 as old and 30 as ancient.

"No, Johnny, watchdogs don't tell the time!"

You know spring has arrived when you see kids out jumping in puddles.

When you hear a compliment about someone, let them know.

Go to the park and swing, really swing.
It will banish your cares and help restore your enthusiasm.

An attitude of gratitude is one of the keys to a more abundant life.

Why is it that most teenagers are happy to do the dishes at a friend's house, but not at home?

Homemade cookies really are the best!
COOKIES

Share *AROUND MY KITCHEN TABLE* with a friend

Around My Kitchen Table is $7.95 per book plus $2.50 (total order) for shipping.

*Around My Kitchen Table*____________________ x $7.95 = $ ________

*Cookies & Muffins*____________________ x $9.95 = $ ________

Postage and handling____________________ = $ 2.50

Subtotal ____________________ = $ ________

In Canada add 7% GST____________________(Subtotal x .07) = $ ________

Total enclosed ____________________ = $ ________

U.S. and international orders payable in U.S. funds./ Price is subject to change.

NAME:____

STREET: ____

CITY: ____________________ PROV./STATE ____________

COUNTRY ____________________ POSTAL CODE/ZIP ____________

Please make cheque or money order payable to:

Traditions of Home Publishing
5134 - 13th Avenue
Edson, Alberta
T7E 1H5

For fund raising or volume purchases, contact **Traditions of Home Publishing** for volume rates.

Please allow 2-3 weeks for delivery.

Cookies & Muffins — Traditions of Home

by Marg Ruttan

Remember Grandma's kitchen and cookie jar? Here are all of your childhood favorites and more, sugar 'n' spice, fruit, nuts, chocolate, high-fiber, carrot and pumpkin cookies and even fruitcake cookies. Tempting muffins, filled with the same luscious ingredients, round out this cornucopia of wonderful tastes and textures. Eggless recipes indexed. Indulge your senses! Enjoy the aromas and flavors of freshly baked cookies and muffins.

Retail $9.95
104 pages
ISBN 1-895292-11-5

6" x 9"
6 colored photographs
wire coil binding